Challenging Racist Language in the Workplace

A guide for health and social care profssionals

by

SAM ILLAIEE

HEALTH & SOCIAL CARE PROFESSIONALS MUST CHALLENGE RACIST ACTIONS AND LANGUAGE AND HERE'S HOW

How should health and social care (and for that matter all public facing workforce respond when a colleague or peer behaves in a racist manner ?

We are going to dive straight in !

CALL IT OUT!

It is crucial for staff working in health and social care to denounce racist behaviour and remarks right now more than ever. The issue is that sometimes we don't know how to handle it when the person who needs to be called out is someone who is "such a good person" or someone who is close to us. The key in this situation is to be ready with a list of potential comments to address. In order to avoid being caught off guard and being mute out of fear of being seen doing nothing, we should get in the habit of saying these. In formulating my own "plan of action," I focused on providing a prompt answer. We must be ready to respond in the same way that we prepare for emergencies.

It is our responsibility to speak up when we hear racist remarks since they put the social, emotional, and physical well-being of individuals close to us in danger. So that they don't become tongue-tied or wind up escalating the tension, we need to be ready in advance with a few reaction options. We can improve our response confidence by creating several scenarios and learning how to react in them. Speaking out can be dangerous, but for individuals who are the focus of bigotry, the danger is considerably greater. It is crucial to consider and act out many scenarios so that teachers may evaluate the danger and the best course of action.

So you need to have some open and closed responses and enquiries ready and waiting in case the situation arises . The number of times I have seen rooms freeze as people do not know what to say and do and that most crucial moment .

Here are nine phrases you must learn and not be afraid to use

"I need to think about what you just stated, so please wait."

"Why did you say that, exactly?"

"I had no idea you felt that way."

"It's not humorous, that."

"I don't feel at ease with that."

"I don't like that at all."

"What! I'm sorry?"

"What you said hurts,"

By having three or four ready-to-use statements that make it clear that we do not accept racist remarks or behaviors, we may promptly confront someone who might otherwise brush their actions off as "just a joke." The intention is to get the offender to pause and think again about their racist behavior. Since the end goal is for an individual to educate and improve themselves, it is equally crucial to have an article or resource on hand for these circumstances.

We can start working toward combating racism and learning to become anti-racist by holding even our closest coworkers or friends (and family!) accountable in this way.

RACIST COMMENTS PUT EQUITY AND INCLUSION AT RISK

Racist comments undermine inclusivity and equity. Even though responding to unpleasant comments can be uncomfortable, they are nonetheless crucial. Professionals must speak out against racist rhetoric in order to eradicate racism. The numerous response strategies, which aim to provide teachers with avenues for further discussion, are not universal in nature but rather represent options that change depending on, among other things, personal conversational styles, situational contexts, interpersonal relationships, and power dynamics. We go over three tactics for developing your anti-racist activity below.

USE 'I' AND SHOW CURIOSITY

This strategy involves asking follow-up questions and making brave and bold "I" statements in response to racist comments made by colleagues. Colleagues can clarify themselves with a simple "What did you mean by that?" preventing misunderstandings. The response can help you understand a coworker's viewpoint and motivations, putting you in a better position to intelligently and meaningfully respond. Additional inquiries help assumptions that support racist remarks come to light, laying the groundwork for tactfully rerouting or correcting behaviors. By using this technique in conjunction with "I" statements, or sentences that start with the words "I think" or "I feel," you can express your viewpoint without discounting the expertise of your colleague. An "I" statement can discuss anti-racist principles or denounce discriminatory practices without making the other person feel threatened, potentially eliminating superficial agreements or general awkwardness.

For instance, "I hear they want to present the award to a black person next year, therefore let's put that X up for the Y award!" What do you mean by that, exactly? Could you please explain your reasoning to me? This gives your peer the chance to defend themselves and potentially reveal or confirm biases.

Colleague:says "Asians have a history of wanting longer hours. It makes sense for him to be offered first.

You say: "Do you believe that Asians have a natural tendency to want to work longer hours? I believe that making such a general statement could be detrimental to such a diverse group. I don't believe it's appropriate to offer advice based on a presumption.

Interpersonal relationships can be preserved while meaningfully disrupting racist discourse by asking questions and making real "I" declarations.

VALUES OF THE ORGANISATION

This tactic emphasises the organisations culture by referring to the company's ideals, which are frequently overtly equity-focused. When a coworker says something offensively racial, you can remind them of these principles and proper conduct. This expressly condemns the improper behavior and, in many situations, specifies the proper conduct. Additionally, it recognises that a person's ideas might not align with those of the community, but that individual still has a duty to act in a way that upholds institutional principles while participating in that community.

As an illustration, you might respond to a racial slur by saying, "In our hospital or council we don't talk about people in that way." You could specifically name a few of the values. In our organisation, we value equity and embrace both visible and invisible diversity. I got the impression that you were disparaging X because of his colour when you stated that. Here, we make use of diversity to empower pupils. When you invoke an anti-racist response that aims to alter conduct, you do it by mentioning the institutional principles, making a "I" declaration, and naming the proper behavior.

EFFECT VS. INTENTION

We can address some racist remarks by acknowledging that the speaker's intended meaning for a statement might not match the effect of that speech on the recipient. You could say, for instance, "I don't think you meant to racially stereotype anyone when you said that, but I think it's important to know that others might read it that way," in response to a racist statement. This method labels the comment as a racial stereotype while framing the comment and speaker as well-intentioned, maintaining the interpersonal bond and reducing any defensiveness. Regardless of the initial aim, this encourages further discussion about the statement's impact and inherent biases

Together, these approaches provide first countermeasures to racism while preserving the integrity of professional relationships. These strategies serve as an initial but crucial foundation for ongoing anti-racist work inside your group or organisation.

GETTING THE OFFENDER TO FOCUS ON THEIR WORDS AND ACTIONS

It is essential to address any racial behavior or remarks made by coworkers. First, I believe it's crucial to restate or rephrase what was said to the coworker. This gives the individual a chance to hear and observe their words and deeds. I next aim to ask a question that prompts thought in the other person. Additionally, it's crucial to emphasize the harm and employ I statements. The person must ultimately understand why their racist words or actions were offensive. My goal is for the person to understand the consequences of their actions rather than to persuade them that they were wrong.

There are some subtleties to how I talk to coworkers on this subject. I want the offender to concentrate on their behaviour and not use my anger or aggression as a way of diversion or deflection. Because of this, even though it is not ideal, I must communicate with that coworker in public. I must also maintain a matter-of-fact tone throughout, refraining from showing any emotion in spite of the coworker's manner. To avoid having the issue turned against me as a BAME person or ally discussing racism with a colleague, it is crucial that I address the situation with tact and strategy.

MY FIVE STEP FLOW ON HOW TO TACKLE A RACIST PERSON COMMENT SLUR OR BEHAVIOUR

I know some of us love a process . We like things in a straight line . These discussion rarely are but in the next five steps your will be ale to see a framework in which you can challenge and respond compassionately .

Your organsaition could use this framework to create something staff could use more widely. Speak to your HR colleagues or get in touch with me and I can support with design

Follow steps 1-3 then decide other you need to follow step four or five. Sometimes you may need step five in an instance. Don't be afraid to use it !

STEP ONE:

OPPOSE

DISPASSIONATELY

It can be challenging to deal with racist behavior from anyone. If you are a BAME—Black, Asian, or minority ethnic—and have experienced racism firsthand or have seen racism in action, you are aware that you experience a range of emotions, including hurt, rage, confusion, anxiety, discomfort, humiliation, physical pain, fear, and grief. Even if you perceive yourself as an ally or an accomplice, you will experience many emotions when you have to confront a coworker about their racist thoughts or behaviour.

Rejecting your colleague's racist remarks or conduct is the first step. Racism must not be tolerated in your workplace. To avoid having your silence interpreted as endorsement of your colleague's discriminatory actions, you must publicly denounce it.

When you openly reject racism in a sensible way, you can select where and when to confront your coworkers about their racist behavior. However, you must make sure that you don't put off taking this Crucial step.

It's preferable if you can address racist actions as soon as you notice them. If there will inevitably be a delay, it shouldn't go past that day.

STEP 2: CONSISTENT TRANSPARENCY

The health and social care professional must inform the colleague of precisely what was said or done that was racist. Because the person is a coworker or because we are scared of upsetting him or her, dont skirt the issue or make light of it. It is crucial that the coworker understands what they did as well as the negative consequences of their prejudiced behavior.

If a coworker is in denial, it could be essential to repeatedly point out the racist words or behavior, albeit this isn't always necessary. you must recognize that if the culpriy t denies using or acting in a discriminatory manner or tries to downplay what was said or done, It doesn't change the fact that the person used racist language or actions. To fully get the significance of what you are sharing, the colleague may need to hear his or her words and actions from the beginning.

STEP 3:

SIGNPOST TO GOOD RESOURCES . INSIDE AND OUTSIDE YOUR ORGANISATION

In particular, racism has been present in our society for hundreds if not thousands of years. Everyone should be aware that racism still exists and that certain individuals continue to face it in all aspects of their lives, including those related to the criminal justice system, the government, housing, and financial institutions, among others.

After you have exposed your coworker's behavior, you will need to point him or her in the direction of resources so they may learn more about why what they did or said was wrong.

We can only assume that if your colleague had known better, they would not have committed their racist conduct and instead would have opted for an anti-racist strategy devoid of harmful language and deeds.

In order to follow up on how your colleague's learning is influencing their thoughts, you should recommend professional resources that will challenge your colleague's thinking while enlightening them, preferably ones that you have already read (a book, a professional journal), watched (a documentary, a movie, a YouTube video), or listened to (a podcast).

This phase calls for accountability from both you and the colleague. Teachers must hold their colleagues who engage in racist behavior accountable and demand that they make the required amends for the clients, caregivers, employees, or members of the community whom they have harmed with their words or deeds. Only by agreeing to educate themselves on systematic racism and how it affects all of us can they be held accountable.

STEP FOUR - REFORM

IS POSSIBLE

Everyone is aware that these discussions may be incredibly challenging and taxing on the individual who pragmatistically disapproves of their colleague's behavior, especially if you are the one who has a genuine responsibility to rectify the injustices that racist attitudes and behaviors have inflicted BIPOC. There can be a need for amicable reconciliation in your relationship, depending on how you two get along. This duty is not on the shoulders of you who starts Process One; rather, it is on the shoulders of the racist act's perpetrators.

The racist behavior of your coworker has been brought to light, and responsible professional help has been promoted. The prime goal is for your colleague to realize his or her mistake, take prompt remedial action to mend any relationships that have been harmed, and alter their thinking and behavior that led to their words or deed.

STEP FIVE - HARM HAS BEEN CAUSED WITHOUT REMORSE

Where local resolution is not possible or the harm that has been done is beyond repair or there is a lack of genuine remorse and reflection report the incident . We must set the example of zero tolerance to this type of behaviour .

SEVEN MORE TIPS

Now lets look at some more response techniques . After all if you are still reading I am sure you would like to add more to you toolkit

1. Repeat the word that caused offence back to the perpetrator. Sometimes they can understand the impact better

2. Explain how the insult was received by you and whether it was intended that way

3. Compare an contrast. 'But she (black lady) was shouting at me' Culture , passion and compassion . Cultural intelligence and sensitivity needed

4. I didn't mean it (often a response to point 2) Teach them that when they offend we will criticise, take it as a piece of treasure to keep so we can self reflect.

5. In my office/ side room/a quite word if you cannot do the most effective call it out in open (see easier discussion. And warn them that if it happens again next time you will call it out . Also take the opportunity to ask the perpetrator to reflect and apologise

6. Email . Construct an email . Ask a ally or support to review it and send it to the perpetrator. This is especially useful in your early days as an antiracist when perhaps the words don't flow as naturally. It will come.

7. We can no longer keep quiet and do nothing. We are currently experiencing change. Action is the key to being an anti-racist. It entails actively taking action to destroy the past and build the future.

THE SPECIAL ROLE OF ALLIES

Staff members have a special obligation to speak out for their coworkers, clients, and caregivers because they are sometimes unable to do so or may not yet have the confidence and voice to express their own self-advocacy. To help safeguard and support, I see it as an essential component of our duties. Taking things a step farther entails making an ally. Allies support, defend, and assist individuals who have been oppressed in finding their voices. As allies, we support the voice of oppressed groups in speaking the truth that others with privilege may not hear.

As an ally, I think it's critical to tackle challenging circumstances with compassion and knowledge. Education can be a solution for statements that occasionally stem from ignorance. I strive to see the best in people and, if feasible, look for constructive intent in interactions or circumstances. Doing so helps me approach that individual with a completely different perspective than if I were to assume malice or overt racism. I can prevent the situation from turning into an argument by remaining composed and solution-oriented. Anyone who has ever looked through the comments on a social media post will understand what I'm getting at and how purpose can affect how people participate. check your own social media . how diverse are the people you interact with .?

Remembering that you are speaking with another adult, someone whose upbringing and life experiences have led him or her to believe that this behavior is appropriate, is one of the most crucial things, in my opinion, to keep in mind while discussing racism. Being an ally entails having the perseverance to continue the dialogue because people's values do not typically grow overnight and ideas, views, and actions are also unlikely to change overnight. I am in a position of privilege to support individuals whose voices have been muted, and doing so is a continuous process that calls for tolerance, perseverance, and consideration.

This is more than just a matter of making things right. It aims to gently nudge a coworker—possibly even a mistaken friend—to realize that their words and deeds affect the people who have been entrusted to them for a long time and have the potential to influence future generations. In my working life, I have seen a lot of allies who are members of the majority ethnic group. The simplest approach to become or become a better ally is to set an example of anti-racism in our reading, in how we live both personal and professional life, and in what we post and share on social media. When feasible, spread the word about anti-racism-supporting publications, lessons, writers, and professional-development opportunities.

Thank you for reading This E book

Sam Illaiee is a Coach and Consultant Pharmacist specialising in transformation health care. He has a deep interest in the areas of Equality and digital

He has decades of experience in health and social care and is well travelled

To contact him email camhssteps@gmail.com

NOTES

NOTES

NOTES

NOTES

www.ingramcontent.com/pod-product-compliance
Lightning Source LLC
Chambersburg PA
CBHW060949130726
48001CB00003B/1137